HOLE SHOT

The Story of the last Mutt Brother

Eugene Coard

with

Robert Blackwell

EUGENE COARD

Copyright © 2013 Eugene Coard
All rights reserved.
ISBN: 1492948667
ISBN-13: 9781492948667

DEDICATION

I dedicate this book to my friends John "Mutt" Lyles, Ronald Lyles, Benny Dunham and Jessie Johnson (The Mutt Brothers) and Drusilla Wilson Lyles.

To my wife Margaret, who was my inspiration in everything I did and every choice I made for over 49 years and 11 months. I also dedicate this book to my son Allen and my daughter Kim, who have always supported me in every endeavor, especially since Margaret went home to be with the Lord. To Clarice Brewer and Sarah Lewis dedicated friends of our family. Barbara Burwell, Mary Gamble.

To my grandfather Prince Eugene Coard, Sr. and my grandmother Martha Coard, and finally to my uncle Easton Gamble, you three taught me very valuable lessons and you are the reason I'm here at all, because you help make me the man I am today.

Eugene Coard Durham, NC

"Wherever you go and whatever you do always respect the people around you, because they are the people who can elevate you. Always treat them as you would want them to treat you. Always carry your part of the load, and never let anyone do more for you than you can do for them."

Prince Eugene Coard, Sr.

EUGENE COARD

CONTENTS

    Forward

1   Introduction

2   From the Black River to the East River

3   From Kingstree to Kings County

4   Brotherhood: The Mutt Brothers Way

5   The New York Street Racing Scene

6   The Players

7   The Quarter Million, Quarter Mile

8   Going Legit (Getting Off the Streets)

9   The Professional Racers Association

10 The United States Racing Team

11 Drag Racing NHRA & Match Racing Style

12 Winning

13 Our Cars

14 Special People who helped our Effort

15 Gone But Not Forgotten

16 Special Thanks

17 What People are Saying.......

FORWARD

Growing up in Richmond County, North Carolina there were three things you had to know something about, baseball, the railroad and racing. I played a little baseball (Little League that is), I have relatives who work for the Seaboard Railroad but I fell in love with racing.

On any given night, one could find a racetrack open, be it a NASCAR circle dirt track or a drag strip. Within an hour and a half there was Rockingham, Sanford, 710, Fayetteville, Darlington, Anson County, Blaney, Shuffletown, and more. Each year Rockingham Dragway would have two major events bringing in major drag racers from all over the country. My friends and I would take off from school on Friday's for the Friday qualifying sessions and return on Saturday and Sunday for more qualifying and eliminations.

Drag racing was a big event in Richmond County and it was there that I developed my love for racing, especially Pro Stock racing. Having grown up during segregation and having suffered many indignities at the circle tracks, drag racing was the most diversified sport I had ever experienced. There were young, old, men, women, Caucasians, African-Americans, Native Americans, Asians and Hispanics all competing together and having fun in the sport. At a drag race everybody was somebody.

In 1971 I remember going to the Rockingham Dragway on a Friday morning early to see the car haulers bring in the racecars. The professional cars were parked in a different area from the sportsman classes. It was in the professional parking lot that I saw a red, white and black Chrysler box truck pull in and park next to the Sox & Martin truck. On the side of this beautiful truck was Ronald Lyles, Pro Stock, Brooklyn, New York and out of this truck came three African-American men, Eugene Coard, Benny Dunham and Ronald Lyles. They worked tirelessly to unload a red black and white, 1972 Plymouth Barracuda built by Sox & Martin. I was so proud because I had never seen any African-Americans in the Pro Stock class. The car was exceptionally quick running a 9.40 ET and 149.50 MPH, right out of the trailer. There were many African-Americans in other classes like, Malcolm Durham, Dee Simmons, John Fogg, Jimmy Spell, Larry Raye, and others but not one in the Pro Stock class.

Hole Shot: The Story of the last MUTT Brother is a very interesting book. It's the story of a group of friends chasing their racing dreams from the streets of Brooklyn, New York to top of the mountain in pro stock racing.

Read and enjoy!

Robert Blackwell

CHAPTER 1

INTRODUCTION

My name is Eugene Coard and cars have always fascinated me and drag racing has been in my blood since childhood. Where drag racing is concerned; there is NO SPEED LIMIT!!!

In the sport of drag racing, a Hole Shot describes a driver who leaves the line first and gets a significant advantage off the starting line. The other driver gets "treed" or "left at the tree". A "hole shot win" is any win where a slower car beats a faster car because of a better reaction time. A "hole shot" gives the driver the strongest start and a greater chance of winning the race.

This book is about a group of guys from Bedford-Stuyvesant in Brooklyn, New York who gained a significant advantage off the starting line by working together. It's also about the people who helped me get a "hole shot" start in life. My mentors taught me that when the green light comes on, I had to be prepared to be the first person to start moving in life. They taught me that if I was prepared and moved first it would give me the best advantage or head-start so I could win in the game of life.

In life, like in drag racing, there are two timers. When the green light comes on, the first timer starts. That's the reaction timer. You have to be ready to react to every good opportunity given to you in life. After your car starts to move and the front tires break the laser beam of light then the reaction timer stops and the actual 1/4-mile timer starts. In life, once you react to the opportunity you are given the clock starts on your success.

CHAPTER 2
FROM THE BLACK RIVER TO THE EAST RIVER

The Black River flows southeasterly through Williamsburg County and the Coastal Plain of South Carolina for 150 miles as it makes its way to Georgetown County where it joins with the Great Pee Dee River and dumps into the Atlantic Ocean.

My name is Eugene Coard, Jr. and I was born in Williamsburg County, Kingstree, South Carolina, on August 21, 1939. I was named after my grandfather Prince Eugene Coard, Sr. My mother's name was Evelener Coard and my father's name was Wash Gamble. My father spent four years in the United States Army and attained the rank of sergeant in 1941 which was very rare at that time. My father taught me that whatever you do always do it well because your future would depend on it. He told me that my attitude is most important and I took my father's advice and always tried to have a positive attitude.

I was raised by my grandfather Prince Eugene Coard, Sr. and my grandmother Martha Coard. My grandmother on my father's side was Rena Gamble, and my grandfather on my father's side was Solomon Gamble but we called him Mister. These are the people who molded my early life and gave me the hole shot I needed to win in life. I had two very good uncles, Easton and Archie and my sister Pansy who also helped in my development.

Early Education

In many of the rural areas of the south like Kingstree, South Carolina we had one and two room schools. I attended a two-room school and my teacher was Mrs. Gamble. She was a very smart lady and she taught us so much that even to this day I use some of her teachings in my business.

Early Work Experience

In the evening after school I had to work. My first job was working at a cotton mill where I made $16 a week. My second job was delivering groceries from the grocery store downtown. I had one of those large bicycles with the huge basket on the front. I made $16 a week delivering groceries also. I always wanted a job because my mother told me that all the money I made I could use to buy clothes and in those days I loved clothes. After working as a farm boy, picking cotton, and picking tobacco we had a ritual we would perform. Today the football player Tim Tebow has everyone uses the term

"Tebowing" but going back to the 1940s at the end of every row of cotton or tobacco row I would pray, Lord help me to get out of this godforsaken place, and the good Lord did just that.

Racism

The first time I experienced racism growing up was as a teenager. I went to Homerville, Georgia to visit family members. On my way back from Georgia I rode the Greyhound bus and the bus stopped for a break. All the passengers went to a little restaurant to get food and the white passenger were allowed to eat inside and the black passengers had to order at the back door and then sat under a big tree to eat. When we got back on the bus the driver instructed the black people to go to the back of the bus and we didn't think anything of it as all the blacks marched to the back. When the white passengers got on the bus they began filling in behind the driver however I never experienced having to get up to give my seat to anyone because of where I was already sitting.

I never experienced racism in Kingstree because when you grow up in the South your parents would only carry you to places where you were welcome. So I wasn't even aware of racism until I made the move to visit Georgia.

Growing up my best friend was a little white boy whose name was Tim Timmons. We did everything together, we would fish together, we slept in the cow pasture together, we would wait for Santa Claus together and he was white so I didn't see racism at that point in my life. However, I did notice one thing. I could eat at the Timmons family dinner table, however if my grandfather ate anything over there he had to eat on the back porch. I didn't question that because I figured that's where he wanted to eat and he never discussed that with me and so it didn't seem out of the ordinary to me.

The East River

My mother was a part of the "Great Migration" the movement of millions of African-Americans out of the rural southern states to the Northeast, Midwest and west who left mostly rural areas to migrate to the city to find jobs. She made a choice that she was not going to live in a place where she could not find adequate work at a decent wage.

Many women moved from the south to the north to take live in housekeeper/nanny jobs. The jobs would provide room and board and $7-$15 per week. The family member in the north would normally find the job and then would send a bus ticket to the relative in the south to migrate north. Many would work for six months or more and then they would ask their husbands to move north with them. That's how many African Americans got to the north. Many lived in a one-room brownstone with a bed and they would share a community kitchen and bathroom with others on their floor.

My mother moved to Brooklyn the largest of New York City's five boroughs where she worked in the dry cleaning business at a place called Reo Cleaners.

Brooklyn was and is a great city that contains dozens of unique neighborhoods, representing many of the major ethnic groups found within the New York City area. We lived in the Bedford-Stuyvesant area of the borough which was home to a large African-American community. Like Harlem, "Bed-Stuy" was a hub for African-American culture, and African-American arts.

CHAPTER 3
FROM KINGSTREE TO KINGS COUNTY

In July of 1955 my mother came home to Kingstree to visit us for the July 4th holiday. and I told my mother when she came home I wanted to go back to New York with her I told her that I wanted to get out of this place so I could go to bigger and better things. I had big dreams of doing things much greater than what I could do in South Carolina.

I told my mother that I wanted to be somebody I wanted to make something out of myself I told my mother that when I die people remember your son Eugene Coard Jr..

So in July 1955 we packed up our 1951 Mercury with teardrop fender skirts and drove the 24 hours from Kingstree, South Carolina to Brooklyn, New York.

When I arrived I was amazed. I had never been to a city that large, with so many people and such a diverse culture. We lived in Bedford-Stuyvesant on Classon Avenue and Brooklyn's African-American and Caribbean communities were spread throughout Brooklyn in places with names like Brownsville and East New York.

I had never met a West Indian before coming to New York and though the largest group of West Indians was Jamaicans and Haitians, there are West Indian immigrants from every part of the Caribbean. Brooklyn's West Indian community is concentrated in the Crown Heights, Flatbush, and East Flatbush, neighborhoods in central Brooklyn. Brooklyn is home to one of the largest communities of West Indians outside of the Caribbean, being rivaled only by Miami, Montreal, London, and Toronto. Some of the best West Indian restaurants and bakeries were located in Crown Heights and Flatbush.

Kings County, New York was a new experience for the 16-year old boy from Kingstree, South Carolina, an experience I was ready to challenge.

Mr. Joseph Unger

I was always tall for my age and soon after arriving in Brooklyn I got a job working for a Jewish man named Mr. Joseph Unger and it was the best thing that could ever have happened to a country boy from South Carolina.

Whatever my grandfather didn't teach me Mr. Joseph Unger taught me. My grandfather always told me that if you buy something make sure it's good enough to sell. He said you should always have something in your possession to sell in case you need some money. Being a country boy from South Carolina every Monday morning I saw 8 to 10 cases of mason jars full of moonshine corn liquor on my grandfather's floor. This was my grandfather on my mother side Prince Eugene Coard. He taught me how to make money. He always made sure that we had food on the table.

Mr. Unger was like another grandfather to me, he knew that I was willing to work hard so he would talk to me and pour lots of wisdom into me. I was a little country boy who was uneducated but highly motivated so he told me the things I needed to do in life to be successful and I listened very carefully.

Mr. Unger was in the shoe business he owned six shoe stores in a company called Lanes Department Stores in Manhattan, and I ended up being a manager in that company. He came to me one day and he said boy you need to take a course in business management so I went to Delehanty Institute on 14th St. and 4th Avenue in New York City in the afternoons and I learned how to merchandise and of course he wanted me to work in his business and I did but all the time I was thinking about starting my own business. I had told my mother that I wanted to be somebody and that I wanted to make something out of myself. I told my mother that when I died I wanted people to remember her son Eugene Coard Jr. So I worked for Mr. Unger and learned everything I could about business.

After I finished the business management course I bought myself a Gibson guitar because I wanted to play guitar and sing like B. B. King. After that I bought myself a saxophone because in those days in most of the Rhythm and Blues songs there was a saxophone solo. Earl Bostic was my favorite and was such a great saxophone player. At that time and I wanted to play saxophone like Earl Bostic and guitar like B.B. King. I worked all day in the shoe business and practiced my guitar and saxophone at night.

I wanted to be a star but for some reason it didn't work out so well.

I even started a singing group called "The In-Crowd" we were a doo-wopp group and we would go down to the Fort Green Projects and listen to Frankie Lyman and the Teenagers. I wrote a song called "Everybody's doing it" and we practiced daily under the "L" on Classon Avenue and Myrtle Avenue and when the "L train" came we would have to stop singing. We were good but we didn't have the talent of Frankie Lyman and the Teenagers. The song didn't do so well but I was still working for Mr. Unger, learning and moving forward.

I learned to love school so I went back to school at BCA Broadcasting Coaching Association school on 62nd Street and Broadway in New York City at night to be a radio announcer because I wanted to go on the air and of course being a country boy from South Carolina I needed to learn how to speak properly. After I finished the course at BCA Broadcasting Coaching Association I was offered a job as a radio announcer in Manning, South Carolina with a salary of $118 per week. Manning is a small town 18 miles from my hometown of Kingstree. I said no way would I go back to South Carolina I will stay right where I am, but the contract with the school stated that once you were finished the program you had to go where school sent you so I broke the contract and stayed in New York.

New York was full of top-notch Disk Jockeys at the time, there was William B Williams, Symphony Cid, Alan Freed, Murray Kaufman and many more who had New York sewed up and I wasn't about to go back to South Carolina because I was through with the South at that particular point.

I don't regret all of my different endeavors because it provided me with an education. When people asked me today did I go to college, I tell them yes. When they ask what college? I say I have a PhD from the college of the streets of New York. Then they ask where is that located and I say it's located very quickly because in New York you have so many different opportunities and if you take the time you will learn something from each one. I learned to speak Spanish by speaking to the people I worked with. I would speak to them in English and they would say the same thing to me in Spanish and so I learned how to speak Spanish from the people around me.

I was earning a good living working in the shoe business with Mr. Unger and in the meantime I had met and married a beautiful young lady from North Carolina, Margaret Rebecca Coard.

After getting married, I bought a navy blue with white interior, 1963 Pontiac Grand Prix with a 389 cubic inch engine and 303 horsepower.

I knew a lot about racing because in the south of my cousins would race their cars I didn't race but I was with them and I watched and I learned. They would race cars like 49 Fords and 40 Chevrolets and so much was learned from them.

CHAPTER 4
BROTHERHOOD:
THE MUTT BROTHERS WAY

Brotherhood is difficult to explain because those who are a part of it cannot explain it and those who aren't will never understand.

Brotherhood is meeting someone for the first time and already having a strong enough connection to do anything for them.

A brother will help you find work when you have lost all hope of a job appearing. A brother will meet for a conversation in the middle of the night because you had a bad day. A brother will write you a note of encouragement telling you how great you are even though you did not get the position you most wanted.

Brotherhood is going to a race with hundreds of other people and getting chills down your spine when you walk in the door because they all believe in the same thing, have the same interests, and strive for the same things you strive for.

Brotherhood is traveling all night to the next race and,

proudly preparing the car together for the first qualifying run.

Brotherhood is living by the same code and seeking to win together. No one can forget the impact that brotherhood has on a person.

To me brotherhood is almost indescribable; it's so hard for me to find words to put those feelings into a language another person can understand. Growing up it was ALWAYS me and my grandparents against the world, so I never had anyone to call brother and I never knew true brotherhood until I met John Lyles, Benny Dunham, Jesse Johnson and Ronald Lyles. When I became tight with these four brothers there was never any question about doing something for each other, but most importantly we trusted each other, which is probably why out of all my so called friends I still only ride tight with them. The Mutt Brothers would do ANYTHING for each other! We were tight and we had fun together working on the cars and racing. The brotherhood that I have experienced is unbelievable.

Brotherhood is calling a brother whenever day or night just because you need someone to talk to or someone to listen to you. He could be a brother you just met and he still shows you love, he has your back your side and your front, at the most crucial times in your life, he cries with you, for you, lifts up your arms when they are folding, and makes you spill your heart out when both of you know you are holding back. He inspires you to excellence, culture, and loyalty to the family. Brotherhood speaks the truth in love and overlooks the petty differences that we all have. A brother excepts your bad habits, bad women choices and bad attitudes, a brother forgives because he is a brother. A brother is constant, reliable and will always try to extend his hand and time.

The five of us were brothers because we were so close together no one could penetrate our circle. We were so close that whatever we did we did together and no one knew what was going on in our circle but us that's what we called friendship.

John "Mutt" Lyles

John Lyles was my friend. He spent two years in the Army and then moved to New York with his wife Cat, and brother Ronald. Cat is a very dedicated lady who was very supportive of Mutt.

We were all from the south Jessie was from Bennettsville South Carolina, Ronald was from Bennettsville South Carolina Benny was from Savannah Georgia and I am from Kingstree South Carolina so we all had that seven mentality and we may have to get along with each other and that's what we did. But the day that John "Mutt" was killed was a devastating day for all of us. Mutt with very popular in New York and there were many articles written about him when he was killed. Mutt was buried in South Carolina and there was a caravan of cars from New York to South Carolina to attend his funeral. The most amazing thing about that was that many of the people that he had beat drag racing attended that funeral. People had so much love for this man that they even talk about him today. People in South Carolina were amazed that a man who had lived such a short time had made so many friends. Before Mutt passed away we had made big plans. We had plans to open up a chain of fashion stores, clothing stores the name was to be New York South. We had planned to open a store in Bennettsville, South Carolina one in Kingstree, South Carolina and in several other places. But none of those plans worked out because of his untimely death.

Benny Dunham

Benny was from Savannah Georgia, and was a lover of Oldsmobile's. Benny and Jessie teamed up as business partners and formed J & B Automotive at 895 Bedford Avenue in Brooklyn, New York. Benny was a great mechanic and a shrewd businessman. He was well educated and kept the books for the racing operation, and kept everything in order. Benny's best buddy was Johnny Walker Red. Benny and I bought a 1955 Chevrolet and put a 427 L-88 engine in the car. Ronald and Mutt had a 427 L-88 Chevelle and we raced each other. We were scheduled to race at Englishtown and we blew the engine. At that time a 427 L-88 block was only $480 dollars.

We were all friends and decided to team up.

Jessie Johnson

Jessie Johnson, Ronald Lyles and John "Mutt" Lyles were all from Bennettsville, South Carolina and were cousins. Jessie was a clean-cut small businessman. His wife was Mary Johnson and was from Bennettsville, South Carolina also. Jessie was a lover of Oldsmobile's. His first race car was a Plymouth Hemi GTX. Jessie and Benny teamed up as business partners and formed J & B Automotive in Brooklyn. The first pair of racing slicks I bought was bought for Jessie's Plymouth Hemi GTX. Jessie had a race with a big guy from Brooklyn we called Big Willie and his 427 Chevy Impala. Well the Hemi GTX could not spin the slicks and the race had been set up so Jessie said he would neutral start the race if the transmission would hold up. He did and won the race. What was so significant about this event was that this was the beginning of the Mutt Brothers using all Chrysler products.

Ronald Lyles

Ronald Lyles was the most successful African-American Mopar Pro Stock racer in history. He was the second driver to break the 8 second zone in Pro Stock in 1973 with a 8.89. He raced around the country with the National Hot Rod Association but mostly on the East

Coast. Ronald won several points races and was a big match race draw, and had several semi-final finishes at NHRA national events.

Ronald was the only African American member of the United States Racing Team.

Ronald Lyles was born in Bennettsville, South Carolina. Ronald's early years centered primarily around farming but he soon found himself, like many other southern African American teenagers leaving the south after graduation for New York.

Ronald lived in Brooklyn, New York and he and his brother John "Mutt" Lyles, worked as machinists at a machine shop in Brooklyn. Like his brother "Mutt," Ronald found himself immersed in the world of New York street racing.

CHAPTER 5
THE NEW YORK STREET RACING SCENE

Big time street racing was born in New York on the Connecting Highway. This street connects the Brooklyn-Queens Expressway to the Grand Central Parkway in Queens, New York. This was such a great area because from one underpass to the next underpass was a quarter mile. This was one of the favorite spots for big money races. Most of our races took place after midnight because the highway was usually deserted by local traffic and was less dangerous. We raced summer and winter any season because we were racers.

I don't know what year street racing began in New York but it was very popular in the 1960's and 70's. Street racing became so big in the 60's and 70's that venders began to set up selling hotdogs, drinks and ice cream to the crowds.

Ronald, Mutt, Bennie, Jessie and I made the rounds or the New York street racing circuit. We raced the Clearview Expressway, the Connecting Highway, 150th St., by the Kennedy Airport Service Road, Fountain Ave, the service road off the Long Island Expressway and just about any stop light with a couple of blocks of clear road ahead.

The Connecting Highway

Everyone knew that all the big money races took place on the Connecting Highway. All the big name street racers knew this and so did New York's finest. The main reason most real street racers like the Connecting was that from one underpass to the next underpass was a quarter mile and the spectators were all packed in to see the races because you could see everything, so if you wanted to see a good race the Connecting Highway was the place to be.

At the Connecting Highway all the racers used the two elevated service roads on each side of the highway as the pits to work on their cars. People would do all types of repairs and services to the cars. It kind of reminds you of a modern day NASCAR pit when you saw how fast the work was done, but remember this was a public street and in the middle of the night. Street racing was an adrenaline rush, and there was big money to be made. So to see the quick work being done on the race cars was an even greater adrenaline rush.

To watch the races the crowd looked down onto the highway from the two guardrails that ran along the elevated service roads.

The New York Police Department would hide and watch cars go by with open exhaust and slicks making their way to the race site. When the police became tired of handling to situation or the crowds became to large they would call in the Fire Department of New York who would come to the Connecting Highway open the fire hydrants and spray down the Connecting from above. Sometimes this would happen every weekend and some weeknights.

The Gathering Places

There were many places racers and spectators would gather to talk about their cars back then.

The White Castle Hamburger joint on Atlantic Avenue in Brooklyn was a favorite hangout spot. We always seemed to have a crowd at our Bedford Avenue gas station and something was always going down in the parking lot of Mitchell's hamburger restaurant on 7th Avenue in Brooklyn, where people would gather to set-up their runs and then they would go under the Brooklyn-Queens Expressway, or to Second Avenue to race. In Queens they raced Cross Bay Boulevard, Connecting Highway and Nassau Expressway. Cross Bay Boulevard was an empty strip of highway with nothing but swamp stretching for miles on each side of the highway.

One of the things most amazing is that someone would print flyers to get the word out about big street races scheduled to take place.

In the 1960's we raced every weekend and sometimes during the week. After Mutt was killed in a motorcycle accident, Bennie, Ronald and I left the streets.

One of the trademarks of Mutt Brothers was that we bought the best equipment, our cars were always flawless in appearance and preparation, as was our tow vehicles, we dressed in sharp, classy uniforms while other teams wore jeans and t-shirts, we went first class.

CHAPTER 6
SOME OF THE PLAYER OF THE NEW YORK STREET RACING SCENE

Rufus "Brooklyn Heavy" Boyd

Heavy was a street racer from Washington, North Carolina who lived in Brooklyn, NY. And ran a business called "J&L Racing Enterprises". "J&L Racing Enterprises" was located at 171 Lexington Avenue, in the Bedford-Stuyvesant section of Brooklyn.

Levi Holmes

Lived in Newark, New Jersey and made a name for himself on the street driving a 1968 Chevrolet Camaro that was called the "Black Knight". Levi raced Pro Stock in his '68 Black Knight Camaro, then raced a black 1970 Nova SS with the "Black Knight" painted on the doors. Levi also owned the ex-MiMi 1969 Chevrolet Camaro. Levi also drove for "Brooklyn Heavy".

Levi was featured in the January 1971 issue of Hi-Performance Cars magazine.

Tab Talmadge

From Brooklyn, NY. Tab was a successful street racer and numbers runner. He purchased 'Dyno' Don Nicholson's 1965 Ford Mustang 427-ci SOHC 'Cammer' A/FX 4-speed car right after Don set a track record at Englishtown, NJ with the car. Tab was a real Ford man, apparently one hell of a driver in any Ford he drove and reportedly street racers would ask Tab to race their cars for them. Tab passed away in December of 2007.

"Super John" McFadden

From Brooklyn, NY. McFadden, also known as "Big John", owned a 1969 Chevrolet Camaro which he had purchased from Dickie Harrell modified it into an SS/AA legal racer. He raced John "Mutt" Lyles of the Mutt Brothers in possibly the most famous street race to ever occur. This race was called the "Quarter Million Quarter Mile". He also raced the car in Pro Stock.

"Fast Earl" Mitchell

Fast Earl was from Paterson, NJ. 'Fast Earl' street raced on 150th in Brooklyn (near Kennedy Airport) and on Route 22 in Newark. He raced professionally in Pro Stock during the early-'70s. He owned a 1969 Chevrolet Camaro (which he used to race on the street and at the track). Some sources state the car had a Booth-Arons built big-block and some even state Wally Booth actually owned and raced the car before Mitchell bought it. He was also a member of the "United Soul Racing Team", a team of racers created and organized by me, Mutt

Brother member Eugene Coard.

Willie "Cam Rod" Campbell

From Brooklyn, NY. Cam raced professionally in Pro Stock after he bought the Platt & Yates Pro Stock 1970 Ford Maverick from Hubert Platt.

The Smallwood Brothers

James and Wilbert "Wicked Will" Smallwood raced both on the street and professionally in Pro Stock. They owned three ex-Sox & Martin racecars: a 1969 notchback Barracuda and a 1970 Plymouth Barracuda and a 1973 Plymouth Duster. The Smallwood Brothers street raced and match raced. In the summer of 1971, they traded the notchback Barracuda back to Sox & Martin for a 1970 Pro Stock Barracuda. But the Smallwood Brothers winning streak came to an end. I still remain in contact with Wilbert who no longer races.

Big Willie Robinson

In the early 1970's legendary street racer Big Willie Robinson, the undisputed king of the late '60s- '70s East Los Angeles street racing scene, and the founder and president of the International Brotherhood of Street Racers towed his 1969 Hemi Dodge Daytona Charger from Los Angeles, California to New York to race Ronald Lyles and the Mutt Brothers. The race never took place when the muscular 6'6" Vietnam veteran Big

Willie and his wife Tomiko realized that our Mutt Brothers car was a 1970 Sox & Martin Hemi Pro Stock Barracuda.

Puerto Rican John Sandoval

John Sandoval was and still is a Bushwick, Brooklyn street racer who was an all around mechanical genius. John built engines, chassis, headers, he was a great driver and he was the go to man if you wanted to run fast.

CHAPTER 7
THE QUARTER MILLION, QUARTER MILE

There is a great legend about a quarter mile, quarter million dollar race that took place between two teams. The two teams were the Mutt Brothers with the Super Stock/B 426 Hemi 4-speed Dodge Dart that had just been repainted black vs. Super John McFadden in a white and red big block rat motored 427 with a tunnel ram intake 1969 Camaro A/Modified car.

Everywhere I go I meet people who ask about this big money race, but it was nowhere near that amount of money.

On Tuesday night the first time we were scheduled to race, the Dodge Dart dropped a driveshaft on a burn out so we couldn't race. On Wednesday, the second night, the Camaro had trouble after the burnout with the transmission shifting so we could not race. Each night we would give the police officers one hundred dollars each and it worked for them. So on Tuesday night we lost four hundred dollars and on Wednesday night we lost another four hundred dollars. We were already eight hundred dollars in the hole and had not made one pass. So by

Thursday night news had traveled and everyone had found out about the big race. People came from Staten Island, Long Island, Brooklyn, Queens, as well as other police officers. We told the guys we only needed 10 seconds so they went around and blocked off the areas so that we could race.

So Mutt went up to the police officers and said, "give us a break we have already paid $800 if we run the race tonight will pay you if the race is not run then you just let us go and they said okay."

Here is how it happened that night. When the starter dropped his hand Super John got the hole shot, and pulled a 1-foot high wheelie for about 30 feet. For about an eighth of a mile the Camaro had about a 2-car lead. Everyone thought we would lose but once Mutt hit 3rd gear, the Black 426 Hemi Dart opened up and went flying by the Camaro winning the race by over two car lengths. The race was finally run and we won.

After each race the police officers would follow the cars through the quarter of a mile, and most people thought it was to arrest the drivers but it was for them to get their money. Most of the police officers themselves were racers however they raced at Westhampton Dragway on the weekends and they knew that we conducted the races in a safe manner. We made sure there were no cars on the street and the races were always late at night but I would not condone that today.

We would always ask our opponent for a fair race, no jumping when the starter dropped his hand but concentrate on him and have a safe clean race. Most people did that and there were no problems but we made a rule that if I leave and you follow the race is on, but if I leave and you don't follow then I would have to come back and start all over. But if I could prove that you jumped and there's a mark or something on your car shakes that showed that you jumped then the race is over and you had to pay.

In all thy getting, get an understanding. Proverbs 4:5

Understanding was the greatest thing we could do when we were participating in a drag racing event, especially where are paying our money and that's why we had so many fair races because we always had a good understanding from the very beginning. All races were set up at the gas station, so when we got to "the Conduit" we knew exactly what each person was supposed to do. We would go there pull the two racecars to the line and from that point it was on, and as soon as the race was over we would go back to the station

On that Thursday night as I said earlier, there were people everywhere and we considered that that race to be the grand national of all street races, the world finals and at that time that was the biggest race I had ever witnessed on Conduit Avenue. People were lined up all the way through the quarter of a mile and probably another two-to-three people were at the starting line.

I remember another race that took place on Conduit Avenue against a 1969 Camaro and at that time each person held their own purse and we were to share the money at the finish line, which is something we didn't normally do. On this particular night after we won the race we look for the guy with the purse and we couldn't find him so we brought the Guardian and there were about 200 people standing around and the police came and asked what was going on and we explained we had raced this Camaro and won and the guy from New Jersey took off with the money and we were holding the car hostage until the guy came with the money and the police said okay and they left.

CHAPTER 8
GOING LEGIT
(GETTING OFF THE STREETS)

We were not been involved in an accident or saw an accident that caused us to stop, but we realized that with the money we had in the cars we raced and with street racing being so popular in New York it was time to move on. While I didn't lose my best friend John "Mutt" Lyles in a racing accident I still lost my best friend in a street accident. After that, we decided that racing at the local track was a smarter option because street racing is dangerous, not only to the drivers, but to everyone in the crowd. I know that the movie, the Fast and the Furious has glorified street racing but it is dangerous, that is why today the police write tickets to even the spectators. Street racers don't seem to understand that they are putting innocent people in jeopardy.

CHAPTER 9
THE PROFESSIONAL RACERS ASSOCIATION

On May 8, 1972, the Professional Racers Association (PRA), consisting of many of the top-name Top Fuel, Funny Car and Pro Stock owners and drivers, was formed. Their goal was to arrange and conduct drag races of a major caliber, featuring only the three professional categories as entrants, and to race for higher purses than had ever been seen in the sport. The leaders of the PRA were admittedly unsatisfied with the progress of drag racing under the guidance of Wally Parks and the National Hot Rod Association, and were anxious to show that they could do it bigger and better.

So, on Labor Day weekend 1972, the PRA staged a major race in Tulsa, Oklahoma, in direct conflict with the 18th annual NHRA Nationals at Indianapolis, and called their event the National Challenge. A total cash payout of $151,000, not counting any contingency awards, was established, with $25,000 cash to each major eliminator winner and $500 per round for all three categories. Jim Tice, who was president of the American Hot Rod Association, was one of the people who put up the money.

While the event featured an unbelievable number of racers, and the Saturday night qualifying session was a spectacular show in itself, we were told that the promoters lost money. Many racers blamed the site, as Tulsa could not provide the crowds of fans needed to make a show of this size pay for itself, and the race should have been held in a major metropolitan area such as Chicago or New York. Others said that the purse was too high and unrealistic, and that their $151,000 cash payout was at fault for the financial failure.

The first race Ronald and I drove from Brooklyn N.Y. to the Sox & Martin shop, in Burlington North Carolina. Ronald and I left at 4:00 am on Wednesday Morning and arrived in Burlington at 12:00 noon. We worked on the car until 7:00 pm had dinner, and headed out for Tulsa, Oklahoma. I started out behind the wheel again and I drove all Wednesday night and most of the day Thursday. I drove to Little Rock, Arkansas. Ronald wasn't feeling well; having diabetes he always had good and bad days. He took over the wheel and drove from the Oklahoma state line to Tulsa.

Those were the good and bad days of racing, trying to get that big pay day. Like so many other pro stock racers we felt we had a good chance to win the $35,000, we had a car that had the capability of winning and all we needed to do was to make it happen.

When we arrived at the hotel I was sick from exhaustion

or from taking no doze pills. We got up Friday morning headed to the track like so many others, with the hope we could win $35,000, but first we had to qualify. All the big Mopar HEMI's were running well, we qualified in the top eight, everything was going well, until Mr. Bill "Grumpy" Jenkins showed up with his small block Vega. On a warm up run "Grumpy" Jenkins ran a 10th quicker than the quickest HEMI. I was sick not only physically but also mentally. At that point I felt like so many of the other HEMI owners, that the big HEMI had no chance to win the big bucks. That little 96-inch wheelbase Chevy Vega with the 331 cubic inch small block was the big HEMI's nightmare. The first time I saw Jenkins' small block Vega run I told Ronald that the small block Vega was the future of pro stock.

Those men who organized that National Challenge Race, should be commended for opening up the doors for big bucks in drag racing as did boxing promoter Don King who opened up the doors for big bucks in boxing. All Pro Stock, Funny Car, and Top Fuel owners and drivers today should thanks those good man for opening up the doors for big bucks in Drag Racing. Even in those days you needed big bucks to put on a good show. Bill Jenkins won $35,000 in 1972, $25,000 in 1973 and in 1974 he won the last National Challenge Race.

In 1973 you could build a Pro Stock car for $20,000 to $30,000 dollars race ready compared to today price $200,000 to $300,000 and you may not qualify. In those days most of the money came from contingency, NHRA payouts were very little, that's why you would see all those decals on the cars. My personal feeling is Bill Jenkins did for Pro Stock, what "Big Daddy" Don Garlits did for Top Fuel. Again I want to thank Jim Tice and the other gentleman that sponsored the first National Challenge race on Labor Day weekend 1972.

Success or failure this event changed professional drag racing forever. While NHRA officials will argue that this was not the case, because annual increases in their purse are commonplace occurrences, racers pointing to the sudden jump in U.S. Nationals round money and purse attributed it to pressure put on the NHRA by PRA. The Pro Stock winner at the first Tulsa PRA event was our Division 1 rival Bill "Grumpy" Jenkins, he took home the $35,000 from the purse plus another $10,000 in contingency awards.

The race was great and we were glad we ran the first one in 1972 but we chose not to participate in the second race in 1973.

In 1973 the association changed its name from PRA to PRO (Professional Racers Organization rather than Association), and even though the purses were high for the races there was a 45-percent decrease in the organizations membership.

The third PRO National Challenge Race took place in 1974 at New York National Raceway. In order to help the hemi cars and be fair, the PRO set the rules for pro stock at 6.75 pounds per inch, regardless of what manufacturer or motor you had, but the 6.75 break included the driver's weight on the scales. This would have made the cars about 6.25 except that the scales read 85 to 100 pounds heavy, thus permitting cars lighter than a true 6.25 pounds per inch. There was supposed to be a 32-car field but 23 cars showed up to qualify.

Ronnie Sox drove our 1974 Dodge Colt. Ronnie Sox blew the 396 Hemi Engine so we installed a 426 Hemi Engine, but with the 426 we had to add 200 lbs. of weight to the car. With the additional 200 lbs., not even the great Ronnie Sox could make something happen.

"Dyno Don" Nicholson, who was never a very strong PRO supporter, did not attend this race because he had a guaranteed money match race somewhere else.

The pro stock field was scheduled to be a 32-car field but there were only 23 cars entered. The cars that were entered in pro stock were:

1. Bob Glidden's Pinto
2. Bill "Grumpy" Jenkins Vega
3. Herb McCandless' Mustang II
4. Mark Harrington driving the Mimi Vega

5. Roy Hill in Butch Leal's old Duster

6. Terenzio Brothers.

7. Lee Edwards' Camaro

8. Rich Simone's Mustang II;

9. Charlie Castaldo's Plymouth Duster

10. Richie Zul Camaro

11. John Rosler fouled while staging.

12. Stewart Pomeroy in the Nelson DesChamps' Colt

13. Joe Varde's Mustang II.

14. Wayne Gapp's Mustang II

15. Kenny Hahn in the Nelson DesChamps' Duster

16. Don Carlton in the Hodge's Dodge Demon

17. Bob Ingles' Vega

18. Mike Fons Plymouth Barracuda

19. Harold Robinson's Vega

20. Bruce Larson's Vega

21. Marino Brothers' Camaro;

22. Ronnie Sox, on our Hemi Dodge Colt

23. Brian Gillis

Everyone was excited because the cars were light and fast with the new weight breaks.

Bob Glidden's Pinto was first at 8.67 - 156.79. Jenkins at 8.71 and 21 other guys.

Round One

Bob Glidden drew the bye run

Herb McCandless beat Mark Harrington

Roy Hill beat the Terenzio Brothers

Lee Edwards beat Rich Simone

Bill Jenkins beat Charlie Castaldo

Richie Zul beat John Rosler

Stewart Pomeroy beat Joe Varde

Wayne Gapp beat Kenny Hahn

Don Carlton singled when Bob Ingles broke.

Mike Fons beat Harold Robinson

Bruce Larson beat the Marino Brothers

Ronnie Sox, driving our Colt beat Brian Gillis

Round Two

Roy Hill beat Stewart Pomeroy

Gapp & Roush beat Herb McCandless

Don Carlton beat Richie Zul

Mike Fons beat Bruce Larson

Bill Jenkins beat Ronnie Sox *

Lee Edwards beat Bob Glidden**

Round Three

Don Carlton beat Wayne Gapp

Bill Jenkins beat Roy Hill

Mike Fons beat Lee Edwards

Semi-final Round

Bill Jenkins beat Don Carlton

Mike Fons, in the Motown Missile, singled

Jenkins won the first two PRA races, winning $70,000 in cash and contingency money.

Final Round

Bill Jenkins 8.80-155.44 beat Mike Fons 8.88 - 151.51.

*Bill Jenkins cleaned our clock with an 8.81 - 152.80 to Ronnie Sox's, red-lighting 9.04 - 150.00. We knew we didn't have much of a chance because our good 396 cubic inch hemi motor in our Dodge Colt had blown a few days earlier and Ronnie Sox was forced to compete with a "big" 426, making the car far too heavy for this race, since it had to carry an extra 200 pounds.

**In what was either a big hole shot upset or a starting-line foul-up low-qualifier Bob Glidden lost 8.73 to Lee Edwards' 9.03. Some say Glidden snoozed, while others say Edwards left without a foul before Glidden had finished staging.

In summation, the Long Island PRO race, despite its rainouts and poor racer turnout/show, was the first time the racer association made money. The track P.R. man sent out a letter a few days later to manufacturers, telling them not to speak harshly of the race because we shouldn't tear down our own sport from within. Then a few days later the P.R. man's boss sent out copies of the contract with the PRO, pointing out how the PRO had not lived up to their end of the contract. It wasn't meant to tear down the sport from just to set the record straight.

10 CHAPTER NAME
THE UNITED STATES RACING TEAM

The Sensational Sixteen
The United States Racing Team

The United States Racing Team was a professional match racing circuit put together in 1971 to promote pro stock teams and pro stock racing. The United States Racing Team was organized/formed by Buddy Martin and Al Carpenter. In those days Pro Stock was the ultimate race cars. The slogan was, *"Win on Sunday, Sell on Monday."*

There were 16 cars in the United States racing team these were the fastest 16 Pro Stock cars in the United States and we were fortunate enough to be one of the sixteen.

The 16 members of the team were:

- Wally Booth from Berkley, MI. 1972 AMC Gremlin

- Don Carlton from Lenoir, NC 1972 Dodge Demon

- Mike Fons from Michigan 1972 Rod Shop Dodge Challenger

- Wayne Gapp from Birmingham, MI. 1972 Ford

Maverick

- Don Grotheer from Oklahoma, 1972 Plymouth Barracuda

- Herb McCandless from Burlington, NC 1972 Dodge Demon

- Rich Mirarcki from Syracuse, NY in the '72 Mimi Vega

- Dick Landy from Northridge, Ca. 1972 Rod Dodge Challenger

- Ronald Lyles from Brooklyn, NY 1972 Plymouth Barracuda

- Hubert Platt from Atlanta, Ga. 1972 Ford Maverick

- Arlen Vanke fron Akron, Ohio 1972 Plymouth Barracuda

- Don Nicholson from Detroit, MI. 1972 Ford Maverick

- Eddie Schartman from Cleveland, Ohio 1972 Ford Maverick

- Bill Jenkins from Malvern, Pa. 1972 Chevrolet Vega

- Ronnie Sox from Burlington, NC 1972 Plymouth Barracuda

- Dave Strickler from York, Pa 1972 Chevrolet Vega

- Bill Blanding from Syracuse, NY, 1972 Mimi Chevrolet Vega

The qualifying system worked different than a normal race. The qualifying procedures worked like this: all team cars made side-by-side qualifying attempts for three open brackets. Those eligible for first place are the four low elapsed times according to car brands (example: Ford, Chevrolet, Plymouth, Dodge, and Wally Booth's AMC Gremlin qualified on the Chevrolet team). Second-place qualifiers represent the next four low elapsed times regardless of brand. Third-place qualifies next four low elapsed times regardless of brand. The cars that do not qualify numbers 13 through 16 serve as alternates for the semi-final round in each bracket. After the semi finals, the low elapsed times loser from that round becomes first alternate. The plan was that by having a backup car to eliminate solo or single runs the United States Racing Team would guarantee that the battle for first place would always be between four different brands.

The United States Racing Team had 10 different booked in mid-week match race events in 1972. The team would go into the city and display the cars and sign autographs a couple of days before the event and the races would be held normally on a Wednesday night.

The United States Racing Team events were great events and were a lot of fun.

The four races that I remember the most are; New England Dragway at Epping, New Hampshire, Englishtown, New Jersey, Capital Raceway, Maryland, and Phoenix City, Alabama.

At Englishtown we were booked for a Wednesday night race and all the team cars were displayed at the Woodbridge Mall. The mall was fairly new at that time and the mall traffic was excellent. There was so many fans who came by for autographs that it was almost unbelievable. The crowd was extremely large for a Wednesday night at Englishtown. We didn't win but it was great racing in front of so many of our fans who had made the short drive over from New York.

The United States Racing Team produced one of the largest crowds in history at New England Dragway in Epping, New Hampshire, was for the Wednesday night race. The crowd would go crazy with each burnout and dry hop. There was so much showmanship in how we put on the show. Mike Fons in the Rod Shop Dodge from Michigan won that night.

On the Wednesday night we raced in Phoenix City, Alabama the United States Racing Team drew a crowd of 125,000 fans on that hot summer nights race. That was the largest crowd ever at that track and it was standing room only that night.

Pro Stock was the most popular class in drag racing at that time.

The United States Racing Team took Capital Raceway by storm. There was a huge crowd on hand, probably the largest crowd in the history of the track. We put the rosin down and did long smoky burnouts and wheelies. The cars were 50 pounds lighter than NHRA rules. Each team made one qualifying run and the top twelve cars were split into three teams of four and we raced for first, second or third place. Our team qualified 11th and we raced for 3rd place an beat Hubert Platt in the 1st round and then we broke a transmission on a burnout giving the 3rd place title to Mike Fons.

Qualifying

DRIVER	**TIMES**
1. Eddie Schartman	9.41
2. Ronnie Sox	9.42
3. Dick Landy	9.46
4. Don Grotheer	9.49
5. Bill Jenkins	9.54
6. Don Nicholson	9.55
7. Roy Hill	9.69
8. Arlen Vanke	9.70

9. Bruce Walker   9.72

10. Wally Booth   9.90

11. Ronald Lyles   9.92

12. Dave Strickler   9.95

13. Hubert Platt   10.04

14. Wayne Gapp   11.11

15. Mike Fons   13.57

16. Don Carlton   15.83

1st Place

DRIVER   TIME--MPH

Bill Jenkins   9.42—146.10   Round Winner

Ronnie Sox   9.38—144.62

Dick Landy   9.47—145.20   Round Winner

Eddie Schartman   10.29—109.00

Bill Jenkins   9.47 – 145.29   1st Place win

Dick Landy   9.48 – 144.96

2nd Place

DRIVER   TIME--MPH

Don Grotheer   9.65 – 143.70   Round Winner

Arlan Vanke   9.62 – 142.57

Don Nicholson   10.22 – 144.05 Round Winner

Wally Booth   9.92 – 137.49

Don Nicholson   9.52 – 143.50   2nd Place Win

Don Grotheer   9.61—104.00

3rd Place

DRIVER   TIME--MPH

Ronald Lyles   9.99 –137.50   Round Winner

Hubert Platt   9.93 – 138.73

Mike Fons   9.45—145.53   Round Winner

Dave Strickler   BROKE

Mike Fons   9.39 – 146.07   3rd Place Win

Ronald Lyles   BROKE

LOW ET: Mike Fons……………………… 9.39

Top SPEED: Bill Jenkins…………………..146.10

CHAPTER 11
DRAG RACING NHRA & MATCH RACING STYLE

A match race is a race between two competitors, going head-to-head, and heads up. Match racing was our bread and butter during those days. The match races paid us between $900 and $1,500 per event.

In match racing the name of the game was promotions and in the early days of pro stock racing there was very little television it was mostly radio and it didn't matter where you travelled you would hear the top 40 radio DJ's say;

"Sunday, Sunday, or Wednesday, Wednesday big match race at the _____ drag strip. Come see the fastest pro stock cars in the country. The wheels will be in the air, so be there." Or you would hear, "Sunday, Sunday, Sunday, Rapid Ronald Lyles and the Mutt Brothers facing Bill "Grumpy" Jenkins at the _____ drag strip come see this awesome show." or they would say, "Sunday, Sunday, Sunday, Rapid Ronald Lyles and the boys from New York with the NHRA Division 1's fastest Mopar facing the man from Malvern, Pennsylvania Bill "Grumpy" Jenkins with Division 1's fastest Chevrolet."

Many promoters and track owners booked us to come to their tracks and match race because they saw us as a David versus Goliath or as the Mohammad Ali of drag racing. Just as Mohammed Ali was fast and he hit hard we did the same thing we had a fast car and we hit the shift points hard and we had a large crowd following us no matter where we raced. We were the only black team who could compete with the major teams and thus we got a lot more races than some of them because there was more of them and us.

We went to Detroit and we were matched against one of the American Motors red, white and blue cars of Wally Booth. We had known Wally for many years. All of the American Motors engineers were at this race they wanted to show how fast their products were. So they picked us as the representatives for the Chrysler Corporation because they figured we were the weakest of the Sox and Martin team cars. They felt that if they beat us it would be like beating Sox and Martin, but we had news for them it was a best two out of three match race and we put that AMC car of Wally Booth's on the trailer 3 wins to none. We felt bad for Wally Booth a former Chevrolet driver, because he was such a nice person and he had just gotten the deal with American Motors.

When we raced at Capital Raceway near Washington DC there were large numbers of people who would always come out to watch us. The promoters were very good about paying us each night. Betty the track manager, would always pay us in a check and she would tell us to go over to Maryland to one of their restaurants and cash the check. We would go in to the restaurant eat spend maybe a couple hundred dollars and leave and later we realized that we were giving some of that money back and we all laughed about it, but that was racing.

Late one Saturday night we're coming back to New York from Ohio where we had match raced Akron Arlen Vanke and as we came through Pennsylvania and we heard a radio announcer announce that there was a big race at a local track and the purse was $2000 to win so we went to the track that Sunday morning and got there before the track opened and we were asleep and the track supervisor came an woke us up. The race that day was a 16 car qualified field and we qualified #1 with worn valve springs. We ran the race and won they never noticed that we had a Sox & Martin built car. When we won I looked over to my left and I saw an elderly black man sitting in a wheelchair, and the look he gave me was a strange look so I walked over to him and I shook his hand and he squeezed my hand and he gave me a look that I've never seen before he was a very proud of what we have done that day. As I read his mind as I looked into his eyes I could see him say for once in my lifetime I saw a young black man come in here and win, and win with style, grace and dignity.

Our home track was Englishtown New Jersey and as the saying goes you get less respect at home than anywhere else. And Englishtown they asked us to pay to come to the track to test our car on a Sunday when the track was already open. We can understand paying if we were renting the track but we were coming by to make a few test runs when the track was already in use. When we would go to ATCO or Cecil County they would pay us big bucks to race but not Englishtown. We never had a match race at Englishtown, it's amazing.

CHAPTER 12
WINNING

Drag racing is not to complicated a sport. Before each pass, each driver does a burnout, which heats the tires and lays down rubber to improve traction. Each driver then stages and the race starts electronically when the lights on the Christmas tree comes down. The Christmas tree consists of a column of six lights for each driver/lane, one blue, then three amber, one green, and one red, connected to light beams on the track. The first, a split blue open circle, is split into two halves. When the first light beam is broken by the vehicle's front tire(s) indicate that the driver has pre-staged (approximately 7 inches (180 mm) from the starting line), lights the first half of the blue circle, and then staged (at the starting line), which lights up the second half of the blue circle, and also the corresponding bar in the middle of that circle. Below the blue "staged" light are three large amber lights, a green light, and a red light.

Once the first car trips the staged beam, the tree is automatically activated, and the opponent will have up to seven seconds to stage or a red light and automatic timed-out disqualification occurs instantly. Otherwise, when both drivers are staged the tree will start the race up to 8.3 seconds after the race is staged, with the time randomly selected by the Autostart system, which causes the three large amber lights to illuminate, followed by the green one. There are two standard light sequences: either the three amber lights flash simultaneously, followed 0.4 seconds later by the green light (a Pro tree), or the amber lights in sequence from top to bottom, 0.5 seconds apart, followed 0.5 seconds later by the green light (a Sportsman tree, or full tree). If the front tires leaves from a stage beam (stage and pre-stage lights both turned off) before the green light illuminates, the red light for that driver's lane illuminates instead, indicating disqualification (unless a more serious violation occurs). Once a driver red-lights, the other driver can also commit a foul start by leaving the line too early but still win, because he left later. The green light automatically shines on the opposite side of the red-lightning driver. If both drivers leave after the green light comes on, the one leaving first has a "hole shot" advantage.

The winner is the first vehicle that crosses the finish line. The elapsed time is a measure of performance only; it does not necessarily determine the winner. Because elapsed time does not include reaction time and each lane is timed individually, a car with a slower elapsed time can actually win if that driver's holeshot advantage exceeds the elapsed time difference. In heads-up racing, this is known as a holeshot win.

At each race the following measurements are taken:

reaction time, elapsed time, and speed. Reaction time is the period from the time the green light comes on to the time the car leaves the starting line. Elapsed time is the period of time from the car leaving the starting line to the time the car crosses the finish line. Speed is measured through a speed trap covering the last 66 feet (20 m) to the finish line, indicating the approximate maximum speed of the car during the run.

Blaney Drag Strip, Elgin, South Carolina

One of our most memorable wins came in 1973 at Blaney Drag Strip, Elgin, South Carolina. This win was so memorable because Ronald was originally from Cheraw, South Carolina and I was originally from Kingstree, South Carolina so we were on their home turf and to get a win was a great accomplishment. We had many friends and family members there that night and this is one of the toughest pro stock fields ever assembled at that small track. Ronald was driving and 1973 test and one every rep. As he got to the finals the last car standing was Melvin Yow driving the Billy the Kid Dodge Demon from Dayton, Ohio and Ronald ran a 9.41 at 144.92 miles per hour to win the event.

CHAPTER 13
OUR CARS

1968 Dodge Dart

We all got together and purchased a Chevy Chevelle. It was teamwork that brought us to this point for we all had jobs, so we all had a few dollars and we chipped in and purchased the Chevelle. We started work on the Chevelle, we put a new engine in and we took the car to West Hampton Dragway and we couldn't get the car to run any faster than 11.30 to 11.50s. At the track I saw the S&K Speed Shop team at the track testing their Super Stock B Hemi Dodge Dart. By that time we had put between $3,000 and $4,000 in that Chevelle. I spoke to Brian from S&K and I told him that your car can run much faster than you are driving it and he said, "of course it will I'm just protecting my investment." I said what are you planning to do with it and he said, "I'm going to sell it." I said how much are you planning to sell it for he said, "I'll take $6,000" within one week we had put together $1,200 each and we purchased that 68 Dodge Dart. Brian stated that he could not sell us the car like it is because the company logo was still on the car so he painted the car black. After he painted the car we brought the car home with wet paint. The car was a

Mystery car and most people thought it was a streetcar with the street hemi engine in it, but it was a professionally built car from the Chrysler Corporation one of only 50 made by the Chrysler Corporation "for drag racing only." We put the car on the street and we had guys from all over the eastern seaboard and as far away as California coming to race us with this Dodge Dart. The Dart is the vehicle that made a name for the Mutt Brothers the driver was John Lyles who was an extremely good driver he was good with the hole shot, he was the one called Mutt.

The Dart worked very well for us and we raced it Friday night Saturday night and Sunday night and the gas station was doing well and we were making money. For the entire time we race that Dart it never went through the full quarter-mile under full power. The car would go through first second and third gear and by the time we finished third gear we were so far ahead of our opponent that we had won the race. We raced 427 Camaros, Chevelles, Mustangs, Corvettes and any kind of car that came against us and we would always win. The car was a 3,000 pound car with about 800 horsepower and that was a lot of horsepower doing that time. We were almost unbeatable

After MUTT died the team decided that we had to keep the gas station and make money because none of us would drive fast car in the streets like Mutt. Mutt was the driver, Ronald was a mouthpiece, and Benny, Jessie and I were the mechanics. That's when we decided what we should do is go racing NHRA a style.

1969 Plymouth Barracuda

We bought the Sox and Martin 69 Barracuda, to compete with those fast street cars in Brooklyn, but the street was no longer for us. Ronald, Benny, Jessie and I went racing N.H.R.A. style. The car was acid dipped, the frame, the doors, and other parts were thin. The car had been acid dipped to curb the weight but then we could put the weight where we want to put the weight.

1971 Plymouth Barracuda

This car was built especially for us by Sox and Martin. We made the cover of Super Stock & Drag Illustrated Magazine, and in 1972.

1972 Plymouth Barracuda

This was the same car as the 1971 Plymouth Barracuda except we changed the front grill and back taillights. We went to the World Finals where we qualified number 9 in a 16-car field, not bad for some street racers from Brooklyn. We learned fast that there was no money in N.H.R.A. racing without sponsorship.

1973 Plymouth Duster

In 1973, we stunned the world with the second eight-second Pro Stock run in history, an 8.89 at New York National Raceway on March 24 in our Ron Butler-built '73 Duster. We would have had the first eight, except that Don Nicholson ran an 8.93 a day earlier in his Ford Pinto at Cecil County

1974 Dodge Colt

From the very beginning of Pro Stock the one red-white-and-blue Plymouths of Sox and Martin had dominated and frustrated most of their opponents.

After the first two races Pomona and Gainesville in 1970, Ronnie Sox or his teammate Herb McCandless went to every single final of the NHRA season in 1970 and in 1971, Sox went six of the eight, losing only the NHRA Summernationals (due to a flat tire) and the World Finals in Amarillo, where his loss cost him a second NHRA Pro Stock title. When Ronnie Sox wasn't winning, other Chrysler racers like Don Carlton in the Motown Missile, Stu McDade in the Billy the Kid Stepp Challenger, and Butch "the California Flash" Leal won.

When Bill Jenkins came into the 1972 Winternationals with a short-wheelbase Vega and defeated five Chrysler Hemi Pro Stockers we knew that Pro Stock was about to change and we saw the handwriting on the wall.

At that time the Pro Stock rules were based on pounds per cubic inch and the small-block Mopar, AMC, and Chevrolet would go at 6.75 pounds per cubic inch. The big-block Chevy, Ford Boss and 351 Cleveland's weighed in at 7.00 pounds per cubic inch, and our Chrysler Hemi and the Ford SOHC weighed in at 7.25. Also to make matters worst, the minimum wheelbase was set at 94 inches to allow the Pintos and Vegas to race.

Around the middle of 1973, after talking to the team we had Don Hardy build us a Sox & Martin Colt. The car had a de-stroked 396-inch Hemi engine to get a lower weight option.

The short wheel-based cars with the big engines proved really hard to drive and in 1973 there were several accidents in Pro Stock. Irv Beringhaus, lost his life when the short wheel-based Pinto he was driving disintegrated at a race in Phoenix.

When NHRA announced the Pro Stock rules for 1974, I told Ronald it was time for us to get out of Pro Stock. We were not making any money and spending money made from our other business.

The new rules were a combination of both wheelbase and cubic-inch regulations. All Hemi cars and big-block Fords were 7.0 pounds-per-cubic-inch regardless of wheelbase. While other cars could weigh in at 6.45 pounds-per-cubic-inch.

That same year Chrysler boycotted NHRA Pro Stock. Ronnie Sox went back to a 1968 Hemi Super Stock/A Barracuda, and we went to the Sportsman ranks to

B/Altered of Competition Eliminator. There was no money to be made so I left the team and Ronald and Randy Dorton raced for a few months and then sold the car to Ronnie Sox who planned to race the car in IHRA and match races.

Drag racing may have been born on the backroads of America, but it grew up on the streets of New York!!!!

                Anonymous New York Street Racer

When you think you know it all about drag racing, it's a sure sign you don't.

CHAPTER 14
SPECIAL PEOPLE WHO HELPED OUR RACING EFFORT

Randy Stewart

Randy worked for Sox and Martin and was the original builder of the 1973 Duster, at the Sox and Martin shop. He work for Sox and Martin, Monday to Friday and would go racing with us Saturday and Sunday. When he left Sox and Martin, he went to work at Hendrix Motorsports in Charlotte, North Carolina. He worked there for 18 years as a sheet metal fabricator. He retired and now spent his time working on our Duster. His motto was "the car must Hook, go straight, and Stop. So you can get out of the Car without the help of the E.M.S service." Randy had a shop at his home in Kannapolis N.C. until he passed away.

Randy Dorton

Randy worked for Sox & Martin, but also started to build engines for the Mutt Brothers also.

Randy was our mechanic/truck driver for three years. He was only 19 years old at the time. We travelled all over the United States and Canada, having loads of fun eating ham biscuits when we lost, and steak when we won. One day while riding in the truck Randy said, "I can build an engine that could possibly run faster than a SOX & MARTIN engine." Randy took a Sox and Martin hemi short block worked on it for two weeks. He cut the pistons put the engine back together, put the engine in the car and we went to Epping New Hampshire Dragway to a pro stock race and set the track record. Mike Fons driving the Rod Shop Dodge, came to the line next and made a pass and broke our record. Randy said to Ronald we wanted that record and we did it. In 1973 we ran 8.93 and back it up with a 8.87 at New York National Drag strip on Long Island N.Y. at a National event that mean we was legal 2982 with a 426 Hemi Motor. We made the first legal 8 second run some one ran 8.94 the Wednesday night before match racing, that racer was Don Nicholson in his pinto. We did it with a 1973 Plymouth Duster.

He also worked for his brother, Keith Dorton, at Automotive Specialties in Concord, NC. That may be where he got his start.

Randy Dorton died in a plane crash along with Rick Hendricks brother in 2004.

Sox & Martin

Buddy Martin was a mastermind when it came to racing and business. He and Ronnie Sox revolutionized the sport of drag racing. Their red, white and blue Hemi-powered Plymouths were revolutionized the sport of drag racing.

Ronnie Sox

Without Ronnie Sox we could have never accomplished what we accomplished there would have been no way. When we met Ronnie he said, "let me tell you boys something and he didn't say it in a negative manner because he wasn't like. He said I'm going to give you guys a car that will win races but that doesn't mean that you will win races, because you have to learn how to win, but the car will be capable of winning all Division I races. He said, remember you have Bill Jenkins up there who is very strong and a tough competitor but I think with the these cars you will be able to put him on the trailer." He kept emphasizing that you have to learn how to win we knew how to win because we were street racers and in street racing you use every trick and strategy in the book, we just needed a fast car and he provided that for us.

Ronnie Sox was the nicest guy one could ever meet. He treated everyone well. Not just us because we were spending money with him but we would always watch how he would see the kids standing by the fence now he would Go sign an autograph he was just overall a nice guy. He always treated everyone like they were special and he was loved by so many people and that's why we always loved and respected Ronnie Sox. His son Dean Sox, brother David Sox and his father are the same way some of the nicest people you could ever meet.

Ronnie was probably the best driver I have ever met. His skills driving four-speed car was second to none. Back in 1973 everybody switched to the Lenco transmissions which was a clutchless transmission. Most teams said they were switching because it would reduce breakage. I believed they switched because they needed to get an advantage on Ronnie. Most drivers went quicker, by about a tenth of a second with the Lenco, but Ronnie Sox's car slowed down with a Lenco. He could shift much faster than the Lenco.

Dean Sox

Dean Sox, Ronnie's son, was very instrumental in helping us put the Ronald Lyles tribute Duster project. He helped us with his knowledge and he even helped us find certain parts we need to complete the project.

Leonard "Bird" Shoffner

Bird was an engine builder at Sox and Martin and built most of our Chrysler Hemi's. Most people think that Jake King built all the Sox and Martin engines and he did but only for Ronnie and Buddy. Bird built most of the customers engines and did it with success. He built engines for were us, Roy Hill, Herb McCandless, Reid Whisnant, and others. Bird went to NASCAR and worked with many great teams.

CHAPTER 15
GONE BUT NOT FORGOTTEN

Margaret Coard

Ronald Lyles

John "Mutt" Lyles

Benny Dunham

Jessie Johnson

Randy Dorton

Randy Stewart

Ronnie Sox

Don Carlton

Paul Gant

Bill "Grumpy" Jenkins

"Dyno" Don Nicholson

Bert Jackson

Mike Doub

Vinston Holmes

Lee Shepard

James Smallwood

Leonard "Bird" Shoffner

Rufus "Brooklyn Heavy" Boyd

I am often asked if I could do life over what would I change. The answer is nothing!!

Eugene Coard

CHAPTER 16
SPECIAL THANKS

Margaret Coard
Kimberly Coard Alston
Barbara Burwell
Mary Gamble
Kathy Dorton
Debbie Stewart
Larry Evans
W. C. Gamble
Shirley Gamble
Edward Gamble
Joseph Gamble
Rochelle Bright Gaskins
Alberta Burwell
Alexis Coard
Tyreck Alston
Cindy Johnson
Rahemma Jackson
Nazzia Jackson
Mary Johnson
Beverly Goodett
Reed Koeppe
Chester Burton
Joe Gillian
Barbara Jean Johnson

Allen Coard
Clarice Brewer
Sarah Lewis
Drusilla Wilson Lyles
Jonathan Dorton
Nancy Wilson
James Brown
Clifford Gamble
Earl Gamble
Leroy Gamble
Ada Sterling
Valerie Bright
Angela Coard
Donte' Alston
Van Alston
Charlie Johnson
Mike Jackson
Cat Lyles
Glenda Dunham
Hemi Fred Ristagno
Nancy Wilson (Hall of Fame)
Dean Sox
Benjamin Burwell
Rev. Henry Burwell

CHAPTER 17
WHAT PEOPLE ARE SAYING

What People are Saying about Eugene..........

When one thinks of their parent or father in my case you naturally say, " I love him." I was asked about my memories of my dad and his racing career, I don't have much of a memory on anything but what I do remember is my dad has always been involved in racing or doing something with cars for as long as I can remember. I remember having the chance to go to the racetrack on several occasions and even riding very fast in the car, always a thrill.

My dad is a man's man, I remember he always had time to take to take us to so many events at school and he liked playing Santa Claus after working all night. He's the dad that taught his kids what he learned in life and what they needed to know growing up in Brooklyn New York.

My dad is a hard worker who I've always thought knew everything about cars and life in general. Today I was asked to write a brief biography and in re reading it I noticed I continuously say "my dad." So many men just father a child but it feels good to know I have a DAD. He was always available to his family and then had time to do what he loved (racing) and do them both so well.

I'm happy he is finally getting some recognition for his hard work as well as such a astonishing accomplishment for African Americans.

Now as a adult I get to make new memories as my dad embarks on another parts of his life while still being a dad always there for me and a great, grandfather always there for my kids and giving memories of being at the race track and the enjoyment behind it.

If I had to grant a wish it would be that so many fatherless women had a dad like mine and that so many people can see his story. And live it through his eyes!

*<div align="right">**Kim Coard Alston**</div>*
May you live as long as you want & Never want as long as you live....

Mr. Eugene has been an inspiration to me in many ways. In such a short period of time he has taught me so much about drag racing and the history of one of my favorite classes Pro Stock. You're simply the best Mr. Eugene.

Marquis Eric Summers
USMC Wounded Warrior
Jacksonville, NC

Eugene Coard is a great person and what he and the Mutt Brothers were able to accomplish during the 60's and 70's is almost unbelievable. I'm glad to have him as a friend and that I am a part of the team.

Larry Evans
Engine Builder
Durham, NC

Mr. Coard your visit to Pollocksville Elementary School was an inspiration to our students. You encouraged the students to stay in school and not to give up even when it seemed that the odds were against them. I'm certain the students will never forget you or your race car. I am looking forward to working with you again this school year, as we here in Jones County continue to "Make It Happen For The Children."

Kimberly C. Bundy
Principal
Pollocksville Elementary School
Pollocksville, NC

My Dad has been and still is the biggest influence in my life. He has always been there for me and whenever I fell down, he didn't pick me up but he encouraged me to get back up and try it again. My dad had a huge impact on me becoming the person I am today. He influenced my life by teaching me life lessons and showing me right from wrong.

Finally, my dad taught me the most important life lesson: how to be a man.

Allen Coard

CHAPTER 18

EUGENE COARD

19 CHAPTER NAME

*Graphic By
Michael Jackson
Norfolk, Va.*

ABOUT THE AUTHORS

Eugene Coard spends his time in the automotive sales business in North Carolina. When not selling automobiles he is spending time doing motivational speeches in churches, schools and other events for children through his Kids 24/7 program.

Robert Blackwell, a labor relations consultant, pastor, speaker, and former teacher. He has had a love for writing for decades. Robert has written training manuals, articles for newsletters, Journals and a novel *"As Long As I Live."* He lives in North Carolina and serves the local education and religious community

Made in the USA
Charleston, SC
15 October 2013